Meet the ...

ANCIENT EGYPTIANS

CONTENTS

WESTERN DESERT

THE PYRAMIDS AND GREAT SPHINX

GIZA

MEDITERRANEAN SEA

CAIRO

MEMPHIS

RED SEA

Ancient Egypt was one of the greatest civilisations in the history of the world. It lasted from about 3200 BC to 30 BC, which is more than 3,000 years!

It started when travellers settled near the river Nile. Over time, two kingdoms formed. In about 3200 BC the pharaoh of the north conquered the south and united all of Egypt. That pharaoh's name was Menes. We don't know much about him, but we do know he built Memphis (the ancient capital) and was later killed by a hippo!

AARRGGHHH!

We have a lot to thank the Ancient Egyptians for.

They invented the calendar, toothpaste — and, yes — mummies!
Everywhere we look around we can see buildings, films and
artwork inspired by the Ancient Egyptians, so let's find out
what the fuss is about . . .

Egypt is a hot, dry country. Almost all of it is desert and it never really rains. The river Nile runs through it, creating fertile land along its banks. Ancient Egypt was only able to thrive thanks to the river and today most of the population still live along it.

Every summer the Nile flooded, leaving behind thick mud that was perfect for growing seeds, making bricks and raising cattle alongside. But that's not all. The river also provided fish to catch and reeds to make papyrus (used for writing on).

While kings lived in luxury, most Egyptians were very poor — even though they were doing all the work! These people, known as peasants, had to work many days a year without pay. Doesn't sound great, does it?

It was pretty hard being a peasant and most made their living from farming. Although the Egyptians were one of the first people to use ploughs pulled by oxen, farming was still back-breaking work.

I'M MELTING!

However, some peasants worked as servants for rich nobles or became craftsmen or artists. These peasants could live slightly more comfortable lives — if they were talented enough, that is!

13

Family was very important in Ancient Egypt. Men would marry young and sometimes had several wives. Women looked after children and the home. Children were considered a blessing from the gods (so they could probably get away with anything!)

If the family had enough money, boys would be sent to school to learn reading, writing and maths. Hardly anyone went to school, though — usually boys would learn trades from their father.

Girls didn't learn to read or write. Instead, they were taught how to look after the home by their mother.

Men and women liked to dress up in wigs, robes and make-up. Cosmetics made from soot and minerals were also worn to cure eye diseases and keep people from being cursed by evil spirits.

Does this suit me?

Wealthy men and women wore wigs made from wool or human hair. Whilst looking stylish, they also provided protection from the sun.

Ash

Comb

Red clay

Henna dye

Make-up brushes

Mirror

Make-up box

Because of the heat, clothes were simple and lightweight, like this:

Jewellery was worn by both men and women, ranging from simple beaded necklaces to fancy gold headpieces.

Men wore short skirts called shendyts.

Women wore long dresses made from flax (a type of plant).

Everyone wore stylish sandals.

If people thought their clothes were too boring, they could decorate or dye them . . . or even accessorise with some palm-leaf sandals!

The Ancient Egyptians were one of the first to write down what was happening. Special record keepers called seshes (scribes) would write on stone and papyrus, telling stories about pharaohs, battles, myths and prayers. That's how we know so much about Ancient Egypt today! The best known system used hieroglyphics — a mixture of pictures and symbols (called glyphs). Here's an example:

This sentence reads: I want my mummy!

We know how to read hieroglyphics because of the discovery of the Rosetta Stone. This large stone is engraved with two languages – Ancient Egyptian and Greek. By translating the Greek script, scholars were able to crack the code and with it read all other Ancient Egyptian writings. Pretty cool, huh? You can still see the Rosetta Stone today. It's kept in the British Museum in London, UK.

The typical Egyptian family home looked like this:

Food was stored in
a hole in the ground . . .

Inside was an entrance hall, a room for social
activities, a bedroom and a kitchen. Homes
were quite simple with little furniture. Not
like ours today!

The flat roof was often used for eating and sleeping in hotter weather.

Wealthy families had comfy beds and mattresses, but most poorer families slept on a rug, or some straw.

. . . but the toilet was also a hole in the ground with a wooden seat over it.

Mmm . . . this'll be tasty!

Ah, another itchy night's sleep!

Ancient Egyptians didn't eat like we do today. No pizza and not a chocolate bar in sight — how did they survive? All food was made by hand or grown, including fruit, vegetables and bread. Wealthier people ate meat from animals they, or their servants, had hunted. No popping to the supermarket for them!

Yummy yummy, mashed turnips!

ox heart

grapes

onions

beer

palm tree fruit

fish

O-fish-ally my favourite dinner!

And their favourite drink? Beer! They drank it every day . . . the ancient times aren't known for healthy nutrition.

The Ancient Egyptians loved animals and kept many pets. They thought animals represented the gods, so tried their best to keep them happy. Like today, cats and dogs were the most popular pets, but they also kept birds, gazelles, baboons and even crocodiles.

Some animals were even trained to carry out jobs. Police officers sometimes used monkeys to help them catch criminals — but you could probably bribe them with a loaf of bread or two . . .

A pharaoh (king) ruled over Egypt. He was also the chief priest and a god, so he was quite a busy man. Luckily, he was always surrounded by officials and servants who gave him advice. Nothing he did was private — not even washing his hands. If he sneezed, it was considered a bad omen. Hide the pepper!

GIRL POWER!

The pharaoh had a Great Royal Wife who ruled alongside him. Her role was also to have many children, including a son to carry on the royal family. Some women were very powerful figures and acted as rulers themselves, but of the 170 pharaohs who ruled Egypt, only seven were female.

DJOSER
(2668 – 2649 BC)
Djoser built the first pyramid,
but it wasn't very good . . .

KHUFU
(2589 – 2566 BC)
Khufu did better. He built the Great
Pyramid at Giza, where he was buried.

AKHENATEN
(1350 – 1334 BC)
Akhenaten was Pharaoh when Egypt was at
its most powerful. He only let people worship
one god – Aten, the sun god.

NEFERTITI
(1353 – 1336 BC)
Nefertiti was Akhenaten's wife, but she was just
as powerful. Even today she is a symbol of beauty.

HATSHEPSUT
(1498 – 1483 BC)

This queen ruled on behalf of her baby son.
She wore a fake beard to make her look wise.

TUTANKHAMUN
(1332 – 1323 BC)

Tutankhamun became a pharaoh at nine years old.
Can you imagine ruling a country at that age?

Homework? But I'm a pharaoh!

RAMESSES II
(1279 – 1213 BC)

Ramesses II built more temples than any other
pharaoh, but they were all made to look just
like himself. What a big head!

CLEOPATRA
(51 – 30 BC)

This famous pharaoh used her beauty and power
to get everything she wanted. She even had her
brother killed when he wanted to rule instead!

Vizier

Although pharaohs ruled the country, they were helped by a huge team, headed by a vizier. The vizier was a special advisor to the pharaoh. He made sure that the people in charge across the kingdom were doing their jobs well.

We can recognise a pharaoh by the symbols he or she wears. If you look at sarcophagi (coffins) or paintings, you can usually see them:

COBRA AND VULTURE
These were the pharaoh's protectors. Which animals would you choose to protect you?

CROWN/HEADCLOTH
These symbolised power. A striped head cloth (called the Nemes cloth) was worn by Tutankhamun and the Great Sphinx.

BEARDS
Most Ancient Egyptians shaved, but gods with beards were considered truly divine. To prove he was a living god, a pharaoh would wear a fake beard tied on with string. Even female pharaohs wore them!

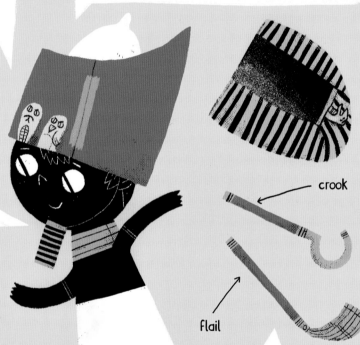

crook

flail

CROOK AND FLAIL
Ever wonder what these objects are? Sometimes pharaohs are seen holding them across their chest. That's the crook and flail. The crook stood for kingship and the flail for fertile land.

Many religions worship only one god, but the Egyptians worshipped thousands. Each part of the kingdom had its own gods too. They were usually represented by animals, or humans with animal heads.

HORUS
God of the Sky

SOBEK
God of Strength

THOTH
God of Wisdom

HATHOR
Goddess of Love

SETH
God of Chaos

KHNUM
God of Water

It was important to keep the gods happy as they were believed to control every aspect of life. You wouldn't want to upset them! Angry gods could cause illness, poor harvests or even death.

PTAH
God of Creation

RA
God of the Sun

AMUN
God of the Air

ANUBIS
God of Embalming

OSIRIS
God of Death

ISIS
Goddess of Healing

Egyptian doctors believed that evil spirits made you ill. To cure illnesses, they would give you something nasty to drink like animal dung juice, hoping that the bad smell and taste would make the spirit go away. Yuck! We also know they performed a lot of surgery using knives, hammers and drills. Eek!

Bird poo!

lotus flower
(for fevers)

mallet

saw

amulet

scalpel

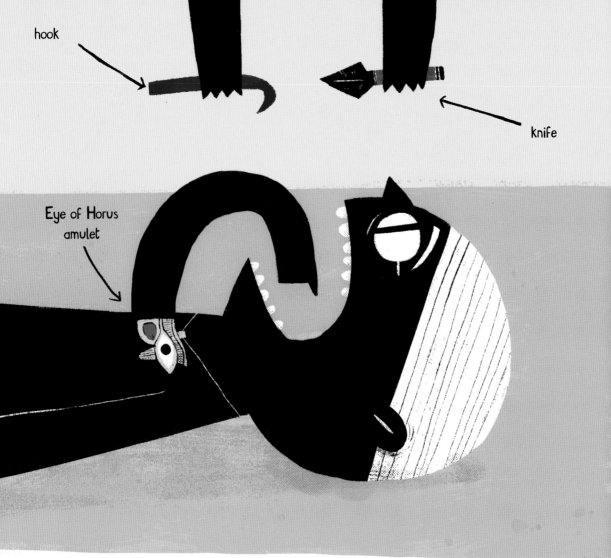

hook

knife

Eye of Horus amulet

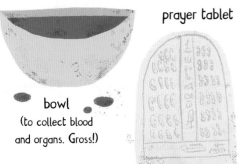

bowl
(to collect blood
and organs. Gross!)

prayer tablet

Priests and doctors worked together to cure illnesses. They would chant and wave sticks around to drive away the evil spirit. Spells written on amulets were also worn by the patient.

35

A temple was the house of a god, and only priests were allowed inside. When a pharaoh died, his body was rowed across the Nile in a funeral boat to a temple, where he or she would be mummified.

Every day, the priests performed rituals in the temple. In the morning, they placed sacred oil, perfume, clothes and paint on statues of the gods. Then they made offerings of food to keep the gods happy so that the kingdom would have good fortune.

Deep inside the pyramids, Ancient Egyptian pharaohs were buried. Tombs were built by teams of workers while the pharaoh was still alive, so he or she could make sure they were buried somewhere splendid.

Once a pharaoh died, a funeral was held after 70 days. The body was carried to the offering temple where sacred rituals were performed before the pharaoh was finally laid to rest.

Er, sorry to bother you . . .

Let meow-t!

Poorer Egyptians would simply be buried in the sand. Only the rich got to have a tomb!

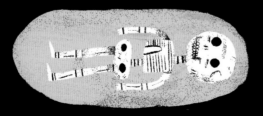

The burial chamber was decorated with paintings of the dead and their family. A false door was painted on the inside, so the dead person's spirit could come and go. Spooky!

Oops!

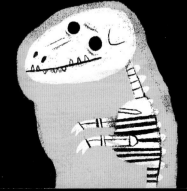

The Egyptians didn't like the idea of dying and just disappearing. Instead, they believed in the afterlife – a place where they would live on for all eternity. To make this journey, dead bodies were preserved in a process called mummification. It was a horrible job that took a long time – about 70 days.

HOW TO MUMMIFY A BODY -- DO NOT TRY THIS AT HOME!

1. Remove the brain. Yuck!

2. Remove the organs. Gross!

3. Place organs in canopic jars.

4. Paint body with oils.

I'm off to the afterlife. Bye!

5. Wrap with linen.

6. Attach sacred amulets.

Tet (protects the limbs)

Ankh (symbolises life)

Scarab (symbolises rebirth)

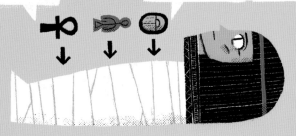

Heard the joke about the angry mummy? He flipped his lid!

7. Place body in a sarcophagus (a stone coffin).

Pharaohs were buried with their favourite pets and possessions. Bit embarrassing for this pharaoh who took his teddy bear!

It wasn't just people that were mummified, many animals were too. Some were pets but most were religious offerings. When crossing over to the afterlife, the gods would ask the dead if they had ever harmed an animal — a serious crime. To prove you were innocent, your spirit could produce a dead cat wrapped in bandages!

Cats were mummified in huge numbers and represented the war goddess, Bastet.

Dogs were popular pets, farm animals and police assistants. There are several Egyptian gods with dog or jackal features, most famously Anubis.

Ibises, a type of long-legged wading bird, were also a mummy favourite. They were dedicated to the god of wisdom, Thoth.

As they are so terrifying, crocodiles were used to scare enemies in war. People allowed them to live in complete luxury because everyone was so afraid of them! When they died, the Ancient Egyptians devoted them to Sebek, the god of fertility and Ra, the sun god.

Baboons represented Thoth, too. He was the god of the moon and of wisdom.

Specially chosen Apis bulls were worshipped as the bull god, Apis. When an Apis bull was born it was treated very well, eating the best food and sleeping on comfy beds. When it died, it was mummified just like a pharaoh.

To the Egyptians, death marked the beginning of a difficult journey to another world where they would lead a new life. This was called the afterlife. If you made it there, you would need to bring all your belongings with you, which is why wealthy Egyptians were buried with all their riches.

To get to the afterlife . . .

1. . . . your spirit would have to travel through a land of snakes and demons to the Hall of Truths.

2. Here, you had to convince 42 gods that you had lived a good life, had never stolen and had eaten all your dinner. Exhausting!

3. If the gods were satisfied, the next stage was to have your heart weighed.

4. If it was lighter than a feather, you were allowed to live forever.

5. If your heart was heavier than a feather, you were considered to be full of evil.

6. A monster — Ammit, the Devourer of Souls — would eat your heart and you'd vanish as if you never existed. No afterlife for you!

There are more than 100 pyramids in Egypt. Each one is a tomb built by pharaohs and rulers for when they died. We don't know why the Egyptians chose the pyramid shape — it might have been to symbolise the sun's rays or a stairway to heaven. The biggest is the Great Pyramid at Giza, built for King Khufu around 2589 BC.

A
pyramid
was a lot of
work to make. In
fact, they were so much
work that in about 1525 BC
the Egyptians stopped building
them altogether. Instead, pharaohs were
buried in underground tombs, such as those
in the Valley of the Kings. We know of 63
tombs and chambers in this region, but there might
still be many more out there! Today, the pyramids are
a popular tourist attraction and millions visit each year.

I've really got
the hump . . .

No nose? We think that the Sphinx lost its nose when it was chiselled off by someone who thought it was evil. Poor thing!

It originally would have had a beard too . . . very cool.

The Great Sphinx has guarded the Great Pyramid at Giza for 4,500 years. The great statue with the head of a man and body of a lion is carved from limestone. Its face was made to resemble the pharaoh Khafra, who was buried in a pyramid nearby.

The Great Sphinx stands at 73 metres long and 20 metres high and is the largest ancient statue on Earth.

No one is sure when the Sphinx was built, but it is thought that it was made around 2500 BC, in the likeness of Pharaoh Khafra whose tomb it guards.

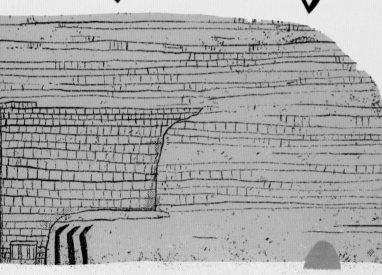

Pigments on the statue suggest it was painted all over in bright colours. How cool would that have been?

The Sphinx has spent a lot of its life buried under sand — it wasn't until 1925 that it was dug out. People trying to protect the statue are worried about the effects of pollution from nearby cities — some have even suggested burying it again!

It took thousands of workers many years to build a pyramid, but we're still not sure how they did it! The most popular theory is that a ramp was built and stone blocks carried were up on sledges. Drawings on papyrus paintings and remains of mud-brick ramps found near pyramids seem to suggest this.

Inside each pyramid, through hidden entrances and passages, the dead pharaoh was laid to rest. To try and stop thieves, workers would build fake chambers to trick anyone planning to loot the treasure buried inside.

Despite this, nearly every known pyramid and tomb has been raided. Often it was the workers themselves who did the robbing! We can only imagine what treasures were buried with the pharaohs, although we know some of them thanks to astounding discoveries.

Nearly everything we know about Ancient Egypt is based on the work of archaeologists. Scientists and explorers have been digging in the sand for centuries, trying to understand more about the Ancient Egyptian way of life — and hopefully find some gold along the way!

Tutankhamun's Death Mask:

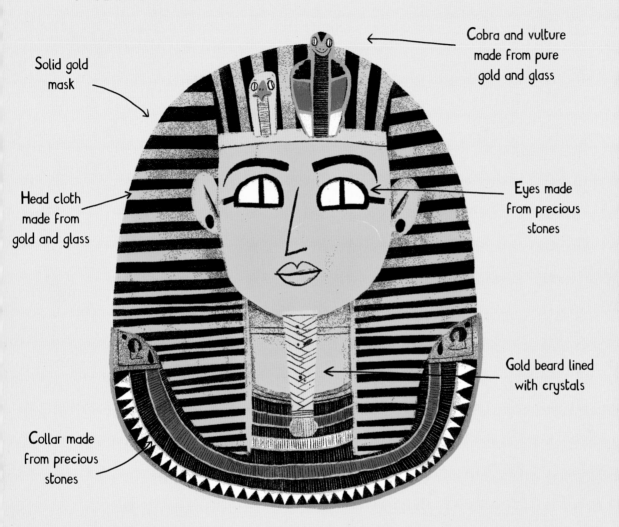

Cobra and vulture made from pure gold and glass

Solid gold mask

Eyes made from precious stones

Head cloth made from gold and glass

Gold beard lined with crystals

Collar made from precious stones

In the 18th century, Ancient Egypt became incredibly popular all over the world, when hundreds of hidden tombs were uncovered. Sadly they'd all been robbed many years before, leaving only a few pieces and some body parts. However, in 1922 an astounding discovery was made . . .

An artist and explorer named Howard Carter had been searching for years with no luck, but one day uncovered the tomb of Tutankhamun — the most famous and complete Egyptian tomb to ever be found.

The tomb was full of incredible riches: statues, chests full of gold, jewellery . . . and of course Tutankhamun's sarcophagus.

But things soon turned strange. Newspapers began to report that the tomb was cursed when Lord Carnarvon, Carter's friend, died of a mosquito bite.

They also reported that Carter's pet bird had been eaten by a cobra as soon as the tomb was unearthed. Could it have been Tutankhamun's mummy? Mummies' curses are only rumours, but even today stories of scary mummies coming to life are popular.

Nobody wants to play!

Despite being surrounded by desert, Egypt was open to invasion. The army was formed after several attacks from the south, west and north. The pharaohs decided to take charge, and often led the army into battle themselves. Egypt soon began to conquer the surrounding land, expanding the empire even further.

Weightlifting

More weightlifting

Push-ups

Soldiers would have to train constantly to stay fit, and when they weren't fighting or training they'd be sent to help harvest the fields or build palaces and pyramids. Phew!

Egyptian Soldier:

Bow and arrows were the most important weapons for soldiers.

Soldiers didn't wear armour, but carried a shield instead.

Archers could shoot targets with their arrows from almost 200 metres away!

If the enemy was close, some soldiers used spears, axes or short swords to fight them.

If you conquered your enemy, you could keep any treasure you found on the battlefield. Sometimes this was a good thing and sometimes not . . .

In 332 BC, Egypt was invaded by Alexander the Great, who was King of Macedonia in Ancient Greece. He expanded the Greek Empire and became known as one of the greatest military commanders in history. In Egypt, he founded a new capital city — Alexandria (wonder where he thought of that?) The Greeks ruled Egypt for 300 years.

Alexander the Great

Alexander's beloved horse, Bucephalus

Well, I hope this doesn't give me nightmares!

After the death of Pharaoh Cleopatra, the Ancient Romans took control of Egypt in 30 BC. As the Roman reign continued, daily life changed across the country. The Roman Empire also brought a new religion, and by 300 BC, Egypt was almost entirely converted to Christianity.

Nearly 100 years later, the Roman Empire was losing power and Egypt was invaded by the Islamic Empire. who turned it into the mostly Muslim country that it still is today.

Egypt today is called the Arab Republic of Egypt. As well as ancient monuments, there are now bustling cities, including the capital, Cairo. Nearly all of the people still live along the Nile, which makes things pretty crowded!

4,000 years later, Ancient Egypt still fascinates us. The history and ruins draw people from all over the world to visit and see for themselves all the incredible things that the ancient civilisation left behind.

6000 BC
People begin to settle in villages in the Nile Valley.

5000 BC
Egyptians begin to build towns on the banks of the Nile.

4500 BC
Egyptians use boat sails for the first time.

2500 BC
The Great Pyramid and the Great Sphinx are built.

2500 BC – 2000 BC is called the 'Old Kingdom' period.

1500 BC
Royal tombs were built in the Valley of the Kings.

1500 BC – 332 BC was the period of the 'New Kingdom'.